My more-than-coloring book about

Christmas

Cathy Spieler

Illustrated by Ed Koehler

Cover illustration by Chenika Brown

CPH®
SAINT LOUIS

⑨ *Thank you to the children at Messiah Lutheran School in St. Louis, MO, who worked hard to give us pictures to choose from for the cover of this book. Each picture was delightful and creative!* ⑨

1   2   3   4   5   6   7   8   9   10   08   07   06   05   04   03   02   01   00   99

A More-than-Coloring Note to Adults

This activity book is more than a coloring book in which children fill in someone's line drawings with color. Because children have their own ideas about how things should look, the design of this book will spark ideas and invite children to use their imagination and creativity to complete each picture.

There is no right or wrong way to finish each page. Crayons or markers can be used to finish the pages or, if children wish, scraps of paper, glitter, or other available materials can be added to enhance each creation.

A More-than-Coloring Note for Children

The pages in this book are not finished. They are waiting for your great ideas and artistic creativity to make them complete.

Have someone read the words on each page to you or read them yourself. Then decide how you would finish the picture.

God has given you great gifts and abilities. It's your turn to use them to make your own more-than-coloring masterpiece!

One day an angel came to tell Mary that she would have a baby. She would be the mother of Jesus. Draw the angel in this picture.

We can use an Advent wreath to get ready for Christmas. An Advent wreath has four candles, one for each week of Advent. Draw three purple (or light blue) candles and one pink candle around the circle of the wreath. The large white candle in the middle of the wreath stands for Jesus and is lit on Christmas Day.

We can hang a wreath on our door at Christmas. Wreaths are shaped like a circle. Circles don't have a beginning or an ending. The circle reminds us that God's love never ends. Add a wreath to this door. Don't forget a bow.

A man named Martin Luther lived in Germany a long time ago. Some people say he brought the first Christmas tree into his home. His children helped decorate it. They used candles and homemade ornaments. Add candles and ornaments to this tree.

We also decorate Christmas trees in our homes. Christmas trees are usually evergreens. They always stay green. This reminds us that God always loves us. Add decorations to this Christmas tree.

Christmas ornaments come in many colors, shapes, and sizes. Decorate this ornament with fancy pictures or festive designs.

Sometimes people put an angel or a star on top of their Christmas tree. What do you put on top of your Christmas tree? Draw something on top of this Christmas tree.

Some families place a manger scene or nativity under their Christmas tree. Add your own manger scene under this tree. Will you place baby Jesus in the manger now or wait until Christmas Day?

Christmas is a time for giving and receiving gifts. We give gifts to show our love for one another. Jesus was our very best gift. God the Father gave Him to us. Use bright colors and decorations to make this gift look like it belongs under the Christmas tree.

People give gifts to show love at Christmas. What gift would you like to receive? Draw a picture of the gift in this box.

Some homes have a fireplace that can be decorated for Christmas. People hang stockings and put decorations on the mantel. Draw Christmas decorations on this fireplace. Decorate the stockings.

Do you decorate the outside of your house with Christmas lights? Jesus is called the Light of the world. Draw doors and windows on this house. Add some colored lights to the house.

What do you see when you look out your window? Do you see colored lights? Do you see treetops and stars? Draw what you see when you look out your window.

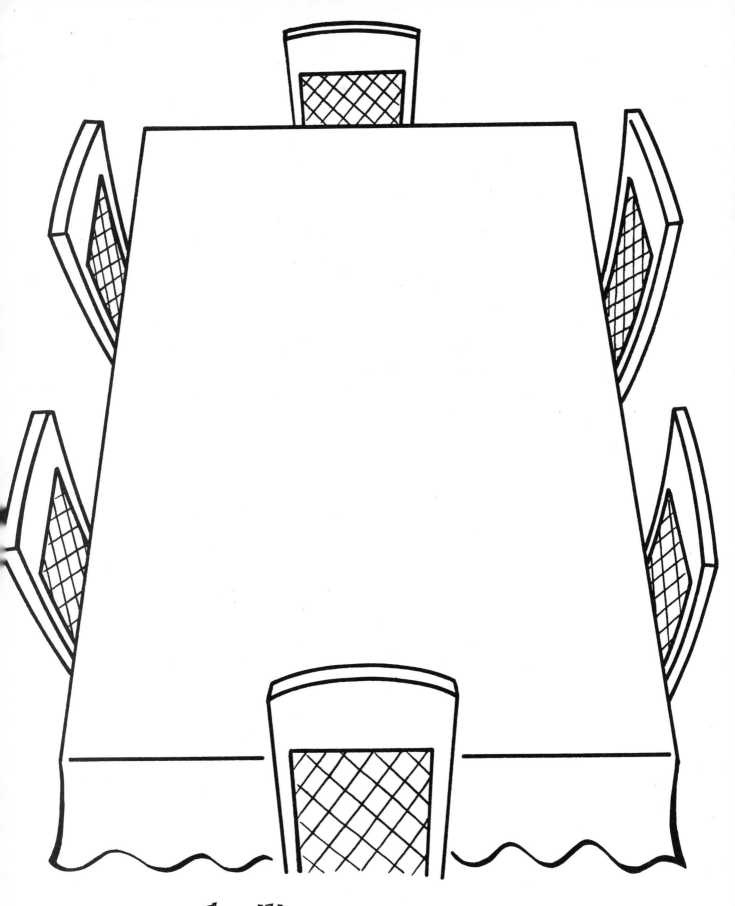

Families gather together to eat special meals and celebrate Christmas. What would the table look like if it were set for a special Christmas dinner? Draw the things you would need.

Pretend this is your plate. What would you like to eat for
Christmas dinner? Draw the food that would be on your plate.

At Christmas we see beautiful red flowers that we may not see at any other time of the year. These flowers are called poinsettias. Fill this pot with red flowers for Christmas.

Do you have special Christmas decorations in your church?
Perhaps there is a Christmas tree or an Advent wreath.
Decorate the front of this church for Christmas.

41

Sometimes churches have stained-glass windows.
Each window is made from lots of pieces of colored glass.
The pieces of colored glass make a beautiful design.
Make your own stained-glass window. Can you draw a design
that would tell others about Jesus' birthday?

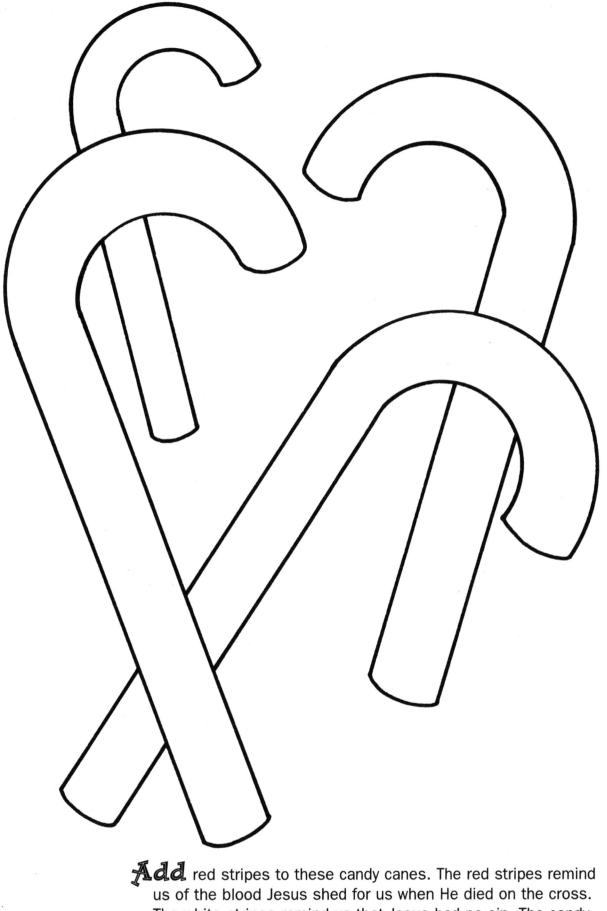

Add red stripes to these candy canes. The red stripes remind
us of the blood Jesus shed for us when He died on the cross.
The white stripes remind us that Jesus had no sin. The candy
cane is curved like a shepherd's staff. Jesus is our Savior and
our Good Shepherd.

In Luke 2:8, the Bible says there were shepherds watching their sheep in fields near Bethlehem. We need more than one shepherd in this picture. Remember to give each shepherd a staff and lots of sheep to watch.

We read in Matthew 2:1–12 that God put a bright star in the sky to guide the Wise Men to Jesus. Color the night sky and add a big, bright star.

The Wise Men brought gifts for Jesus. If this was a gift for Jesus, what would it look like? Would it have jewels and fancy designs? Decorate the treasure chest for Jesus.

Our heads are filled with many thoughts at Christmas.
Draw what you think this child is dreaming about.

At Christmas, we send beautiful cards to loved ones to share our joy. Design a Christmas card to send to a friend. Draw a picture that tells your friend it is Jesus' birthday.

If you could make a gift for someone, what would it be?
Draw the gift you would make in this space.

59

We celebrate the birth of Jesus, our Savior, at Christmas. In this picture, Mary and Joseph are watching over baby Jesus. Draw baby Jesus in the manger. Add animals and shepherds too.

What will your family look like as you celebrate the birthday of Jesus this Christmas? Draw your family in this picture frame. Thank God that He sent Jesus to be born on the first Christmas for you and your family!

The End